Praise

"It's common wisdom that there are no adequate words to describe the depth and complexity of grief. Yet in this stunning work, Miguel Eichelberger manages to excavate his own experience of grief and transform it into exquisite language that makes anyone who has ever grieved—in short, everyone—feel seen and known. With an unflinching yet compassionate eye on his own interiority and the way it connects him to his fellow humans, he guides us through the landscape of pain and the gifts that are buried within it. This is a collection that will remind you that you are not alone, even when you are missing someone with all your heart, and that will make you feel grateful to be alive, even when that life is difficult."

—Stephanie Harrison, *New York Times* best-selling author of *The New Happy*

"In Miguel Eichelberger's *Everything Is*, we are given poems both clear-eyed and unafraid to wear their heart on their sleeve. With honesty and surprise, Eichelberger takes us through grief's most tender and most clinical moments, the poems working together like light on faceted glass, culminating in a collection that shines."

—Donna Kane, author of *Orrery*, a finalist for the Governor General's Award

Praise

"Miguel Eichelberger's *Everything Is* is a book of love poems about the loss of his father. For those of us who have experienced such loss, Eichelberger evokes the deeply familiar disembodiment, the slow unwinding of the first minutes and hours. He takes us back to the place where we first begin that long wait for forgetting, the fading of details, the healing of grief. I had not thought I would ever want to go back, but the intimate, graceful shock of these poems allows it. Imagine my gratitude to discover that I have not forgotten. Not at all."

—Mark Greene, author of *Remaking Manhood: Stories From the Front Lines of Change*

Everything Is

Everything
Is

―❈―

by

Miguel Eichelberger

Copyright © 2025 by Miguel Eichelberger

All rights reserved.

Paperback ISBN: 978-1-64672-361-4

eBook ISBN: 978-1-64672-366-9

Published by Poetose

Boston, MA

Illustrated by Sara Zieve Miller

First Edition

To reprint, reproduce, or transmit electronically, or by recording all or part of this manuscript, beyond brief reviews or educational purposes, please send a written request to Poetose.

www.poetose.com

Contents

Reflections on the Carrion Sidewalk 1
Loss 2
At a Body's Bedside 3
Self-Talk at the Wake 5
Watching Mourners 6
Restless 8
Carrying Dad's Ashes Back to Switzerland 9
Reflections After the First Full Sleep in Weeks 10
Remember to Rest 11
On the Urge to Do Something 12
On What Loss Might Be For 13
Rummaging Through Old Boxes 14
On Reading the Literature 15
Odd Things at Odd Times Undo You 17
You Lose a Lot of Sleep 18
Reflections on Nature's Design Skill 19
Beyond the Light of the Fire 20
How Purpose Communicates 22
On the Return to Living 23
Reflecting on "Come as Quick as You Can" 24
Grief Makes Us Explorers 25
How It Probably Went at the Hospital, Knowing Dad . . . 26
On Mortality 27
Get on with It Then 28
Acknowledgements 29
About the Author 31

For my dad, Max Eichelberger
(July 24, 1942 – April 23, 2017).

For my mom, and my siblings.

And me.

And you.

Reflections on the Carrion Sidewalk

Bee husks and roadkill
raccoons, on a sun-etched Sunday, are easy
to walk on by. Dad's death caught
me dreaming and comfortable like that.

There's no way to step past an assurance
so complete, completely decimated. The bees
will recover, right? Sure, raccoons are plenty
and besides they wreck the trashcans.

Him though? What do you mean he doesn't
answer the phone tomorrow, or any other day
of sunrise-certainty, with a smile you can hear?

There will likely be a supernova
visible to our limited eyes sometime this decade.
They know because it cycles, returns
every eighty years or so. I don't need
to let go of false securities, this always-state,
or him, do I?

I'll say I'm happy. I'll say I'm whole. And the bees
will recover.

Loss

is a wound that bleeds out,
    and keeps bleeding.
It won't matter, the strength of your hands.
The pressure
    supposed to be keeping,
    the blood where it matters, disbands.

And there's Grief in his ugly tuxedo,
    all rumpled
    and never in style.
When the fucker comes in for the evening,
    he hints
    that he might stay a while.

At a Body's Bedside

I've known no quiet as empty or full
as a hospital room whose machinery
has gone silent.

It mimics the body in the bed—
compounds its quality.
Ambiguity died too. He's gone.
Full stop. No dispute.

This quiet bursts with novel truths:
he won't be using that rigid hand.
That feels like a new sentence.

I start talking out loud. Maybe
to stem the quiet, maybe because
I've seen it before, people talking
to empty bodies, and I've fallen
to the level of my training for this.

I say the important things that he knew,
back when he was still making dinner
or teaching me the world from
his black pleather chair.

Like the room, some vital piece, an inhabitant,
is not with me anymore. I can't consult
or need him anymore.

This quiet is a too-full cup,
spilling awful lessons. Obvious now
as they put sudden life in old platitudes,
and say loud, for the first time:

Self-Talk at the Wake

Don't mind that odd feeling of easy breaking;
    that card-house quiet of held breath.

The photo hits harder than the casket.

Watching Mourners
(sung to the tune of *One of Us Cannot Be Wrong* by Leonard Cohen)

I can't understand the small candles
that mourners set burning in loss.
They push back the darkness in flickers,
but that border no candle can cross.

Is a wisp of soft light to the longest of nights
any more than a thing to consume?
Their signals all end in the prayers that we lend
to the ageless echoes of the room.

A widow bends forward to kiss him.
A young son leans closer to see.
They each hold a peace that is ruined,
and fools say is mended in grief.

The candle's brave light won't return a lost life
and its monument burns down to smoke.
It lives like the man who has gone to the land
where the lighthouse can't call back the boat.

I'm mired in the long meditations
that bring the mind nearer some dream.
A vision of sweet visitations that
convince me my father is free.

And I know they don't work
and this new kind of hurt
is a burden you can't leave behind.

The flame's just a wish
not a lantern for this
strange passage no map can define.

Restless

Ghosts aren't real, says a numbed tongue and
stilt-lipped voice somewhere in my mind. I
stand mid-night, mid-world in my childhood

living room, squinting for apparitions.
I used to sit cross-legged on that floor. Rest
isn't real, and sleep, who knows

what that even means, lifting trinkets and examining
mantle photos. I take in whatever the limit
is on a mind in this. The buzz,

like I slept on my amygdala wrong. Waiting
for recirculation in the parts for feeling,
for spider-crawl sensation.

No ghost, just me and small monuments,
small-eyeing photos of myself,
I want nothing

to do with that whole person. That photo
of a young man grinning, feeling
the flattened red carpet underfoot.

Carrying Dad's Ashes Back to Switzerland

The security scale tells the account:
pounds, kilograms, inches, meters, those
measures that used to matter mean nothing
to a collection of cinders. It's all burned
in the end to ash.
Residue that the wind could take
makes the lifeless TSA employee ask
questions, and requires paperwork, more
paperwork than a blood-moving person just
to return to a homeland's dust.
They're what's left of my father, I say,
and I wonder what special freight
you were tasked to carry into
the dark places of this world, security guard,
before ever you breathed outside your mother.

These are my dad. Echoes of cosmic spark,
the remainders of fire. Now you know.

Reflections After the First Full Sleep in Weeks

After detonation and flash-shock and sudden-death
silence. After consulting with the priors of a faith
you do not share. After crying so hard you begin
to understand a word like Endless. After letting
the silverfish live for the first time ever. After
wondering if the heart-sore clench is permanent
the eye breaks open to a daylight that sings, chants
rise-set, and a dust-and-blood finger flexes above
the rubble that used to look like you. Then
a hum of coming pain. A convulsion of the lung.
Now the heartbeat in the eardrum. In the head. And
the keeping-on fever breaks, with deaths of all kinds
everywhere. What happened
to routine, and choice, you wonder, like reading
a casualty list. Oh, I see.
I see.
After all that, when the loneliness that
only survivors know overcasts colors you
forget how to appreciate, and love—
after that, help might be
the only thing you can find.

Remember to Rest

By now, some of the swelling
has eased, keep pressing ice
against it, taking ibuprofen that only
sort-of does the trick.

I think of a forest, bristling with shrieks and
crenelating sensations, something
like prey, and wolves somewhere,
and the explorer needing heat, or lenient shelter.

I think of sitting on the rough trunk
of a downed tree, confused by distance
and breathing in time with life's pursuit.
No matter what might kill you.

On the Urge to Do Something

There're mice in the traps and why
should I clean, tamp the rugs, scrub
down the bathroom, run around in
a little make-believe like this place
always looks like that, shine
and magazine-cover?

No. I'll take this clastic chaos as it is, dusty
windows and smudged light switches,
rodent company. Let it be a moment
like any other, with a little mud on the floors.

I get the idea, the psychology of it, but reality
isn't clean, nowhere near, and I don't think
it ever was or could be like that. This
isn't me avoiding anything. I think,
it's more like a surrender or maybe patience.

Clean will earn its way home, ultimately,
while I go on lurching
inch to inch, somewhere I'm supposed to be
again.

On What Loss Might Be For

A more enlightened person might say grief
makes promises it has no intention to keep—
because it can't. He might say

there's something worth it in those pink lines
on the skin, or in the loose-change jangle
of tired joints.

To me, it's a thing of movement,
equal-and-opposite momentum, I write here
and think there, and feel somewhere else,

and that sets off some hidden genetic process
of accepting that the dead are deaf and mute
and it's beautiful.

So I write a noonday pond. I scratch
a dying marsh, and quote a classic, hunting
in old minds, then my mind. And maybe

that is the dead teaching us to write poems.
All of these words are theirs
probably.

I pick up the phone to chat about it,
and put it down when I remember.

Rummaging Through Old Boxes

is like gathering to a barker
at the afterlife bazaar.

Like sauntering amid the wonders of a life
filled to bursting. Shelves lined with tinctures of moments,
and you begin to understand how a life gets filled
with all the same things as the last.

Longing here, obsessions and regret over there,
awards and honors. Black-and-white moments,
found as if by archaeology, the story trying to
tell itself somehow, and you fill in the blanks.

Curios of survival and crime hocked
and in this box, life lived. In that one, taken.
You standing there gawking are life made.

Truths, embellishments, wounds open and shut
and you realize that no experience can be shared
because of where experience is experienced.

And that mind is gone.
Elsewhere if one believes that sort of thing,
and nowhere.

On Reading the Literature

Psychologically speaking, it really is
all part of the process. Everything is.

Like cells in the inflammatory response
racing to the injury, anxiously toiling
to reconstruct—an amateur painter
called to restore the Mona Lisa—she's
a bit off here, scar tissue

breaks easier. I read that patience
sees off the bone-closet stink
of kept traumas. I read that healing
never goes one way.

I am a hummingbird, a planet, a shark.
I must move, but I've been an idle heart
beating just to keep the lamps lit. And

that's part of it too. I am a laborer,
a singing spade set to and stomped
through earth's flesh, torture
burning the shoulders and

comedy, that's part of it too, you laugh
with the open blisters and worming soil
everywhere tasting the meat of the world,

the history of the world. Digging through anything that can take it.

So far it all reads similar, but I'll see what the next researcher says.

Odd Things at Odd Times Undo You

On the bus halfway to work, the memory
strobes, a seizure, picks me clean—
you laying there, head awry, slack and empty,
tilting up and away. My father,
the mannequin.

The ground was never stable anywhere,
and that's fine.

The blush and climate change
of a hard cry, and what a privilege,
a gift, to love like this, like a story.

I say *thank you*, and the driver
asks if I'm all right.

You Lose a Lot of Sleep

but something about the night,
and your feet being the only ones
in the grass, has the landscape
smelling of flowers, humming
of night-time bothered insects,
and the wounds don't look as mean.

Douglas Firs recognize their young,
they share their carbon resources
with each other through the root
and soil, ensuring that always more
goes to trees that grew from their seeds.

Considering that, I could feel lonelier
than the last iteration of a species.

Instead I write:

> *Though monuments grow fewer there is hope*
> *Though my love was never certain, I still wrote*
> *Though I left a burning harbor with no boat*
> *I learned that any fool can learn to float*

Reflections on Nature's Design Skill

The senses are the openings
nature gives the world to invade us.
There's no order to it that I can see.

Whichever ingress is ready, or weakest I suppose.
I think taste came first, for a time it's just consuming
then flavor again from nowhere.

Things like desire and ambition,
like I was walking toward them over
some great distance, clarified themselves

eventually. Maybe nature designed
it this way, so that reliving would be more
manageable. It's not a blind man

regaining his sight, more like
a first-time skydiver, looking
away from the open door.

Beyond the Light of the Fire

Wildlife scatter. Lakes shudder.
Leaves turn their light
sides to the rain.

It starts below consciousness,
somewhere truer than anger or fear,
and inflates the mind's quiet
to bursting.

It comes from the middle, this howl
that moves fast over land and sea. Trees
bend with the shock, roots up and swept
to a scream that pulls us primitive
beyond the light of the fire.

It's the gasp that stops the drowning,
a last-moment antidote.
It's every single story's subject

what we've always been getting at,
known well to a child, and the dirt,
often dismissed by age.

Some say it peels you to the meat,
use good words, epiphany, vocation.
I think it's where real power waits.

You only start to hear it, violent,
undeterred by our deterrences,
when the numbness goes thin enough

and you step out ginger to meet it.

How Purpose Communicates

just go it says
and then we move
we know not what
we do.
we do.

we learn them then
the skills and truths
and then it says:
Here's proof.
Here's proof.

On the Return to Living

There is no ceremony.
It's quiet.
The return is quiet.

The people looking at their shoes
are doing the best they can.

And so are you.

Reflecting on "Come as Quick as You Can"

The last time I took this flight
    the fog was viscous.
I despised airplane mode waiting
    for word about dad.
A child seeing tears on my cheek
    gave me her grin.
An agent at the gate
    gave me her thanks.
I learned the great suffering
    of knowing before you know.
I tasted my first lick
    at real defeat.
I was tired, I was drunk
    on staying strong.
I was lit up
    by a slow-approaching end.
I used to like waiting
    for a flight.
The last time I came around
    my brother told me dad was gone.

Grief Makes Us Explorers

You don't make peace.
It doesn't work like that.

I notice things like peace,
things like breath, things that are there.

Beneath sound and machine and schedule
they don't disappear.

Your heart's been beating.
This whole time, it's been working,
waiting for you to be able
to notice it again.

It knew you would go looking.

How It Probably Went at the Hospital, Knowing Dad

They marveled at his genius
    while tending to his bed.
They gathered words and speeches
    all those charming things he said:
    "My friends, I don't need aegis.
    The reaper's shores are my beachhead."

They spoke about his courage
    asked him if he feared the end:
"Fear is a position
    only cowards would defend.
    If these are my last minutes
    tell them play that song again
    and send around the server,
    ask what drink she recommends."

On Mortality

Here's the joke—
grief's lessons are simple

One: how to die.
Two: how to live.
Three: how to feel.
Four: the priest prays too.
Five: life is a joyful mutiny.
Six: and so is death.

Oh, and all of us
are better than okay.

Get on With It Then

you go on finding poems then
go on—go on

you cut cold stones for diadems
go on—go on

some person sells the lovely gems
a song—a song

and yeah, you might buy here again
move on—move on

you live like it may never end
hold on—hold on

you stop dividing joy from sin
it's gone—it's gone

you make art no one ever did
a song—a song

that fight you hope to never win
is on—you're on

Acknowledgements

Poems in this collection have, in one form or another, previously appeared in *Harpur Palate*, *Plainsongs Magazine*, and *Soliloquies Anthology*. I'm beyond grateful to every literary magazine that has supported my work over the years, but to these three especially, a huge thanks.

I don't believe we're lucky in the opportunities that come our way, but in the people who support us when they do. I'm lucky. Very lucky. To those who believed, gave their time, inspired, read, re-read, re-re-read and provided feedback both scathing and encouraging, know that I'm grateful.

Here're a few of you:

Rita Eichelberger (mom), Paulo Eichelberger (brother), Anna Eichelberger (sister), Robert Eichelberger (also brother). Donna Kane, one of the best Canadian poets doing it at the moment. Keith Kennedy, an uncommon creator and friend. Will Richter, exceptional writer, editor and friend. Anthony Santiago

& Alexis Kellum-Creer, incredible humans and artists. Liz McMullen, the only reason my words graced stages across the UK. Allison Duthie & Joel Goundry, family at a distance. Ben Yu Schott, the lightning rod that accidentally and profoundly unlocked the answer to this collection.

A massive thank you to Meia Geddes who chose to publish this chapbook. It's a joy that these words ended up here.

And more luck still (or whatever is greater than luck), Kerianne Cameron. The best editor, reader, writer and life-accomplice a highwayman could ever hope to know—every word and caesura mean more because of your fingerprints. Let's slip out the back.

Natalia and Max: you curious, adventurous, dangerous originals, please keep breaking and creating things. Never settle for less. The world ain't ready for you.

One final thanks to the best man I ever knew—faults and gifts included—my father, Max Eichelberger. Big shoes to fill, tough act to follow, dangerous to the wicked, missing from the line. I'll do my best to hold his position knowing I could never hold it like him.

About the Author

Miguel Eichelberger is a writer, communicator, and joyful mutineer. He received his BA in English at the University of Calgary with concentrations in Archaeology and Theatre. His creative work has appeared in literary magazines and on stages around the world. His most recent publications include *Acta Victoriana*, *Harpur Palate*, *Rappahannock Review*, *Literary Review of Canada*, and *Plainsongs Magazine*, and his poetry is a feature piece in the *Ducktown Poetry Trail* in Atlantic City, a collaborative art project between Murphy Writing and the Noyes Museum of Art of Stockton University that brings awareness to issues of social justice. He also has a screenplay optioned in Ireland.

www.ingramcontent.com/pod-product-compliance
Lightning Source LLC
Chambersburg PA
CBHW030536080526
44585CB00014B/967